# DO PLANTS EAT MEAT?
## THE WONDERFUL WORLD OF CARNIVOROUS PLANTS

Biology Books for Kids
Children's Biology Books

**BABY PROFESSOR**
EDUCATION KIDS

Speedy Publishing LLC
40 E. Main St. #1156
Newark, DE 19711
www.speedypublishing.com
Copyright 2017

All Rights reserved. No part of this book may be reproduced or used in any way or form or by any means whether electronic or mechanical, this means that you cannot record or photocopy any material ideas or tips that are provided in this book

People eat meat and plants, and so do animals. But do plants ever eat meat? Could a plant eat a person? Read on, and let's find out!

**Venus Flytrap**

# MEAT-EATING PLANTS

Yes, there are meat-eating plants. But none of them are big enough or fast enough to take a bite out of you!

Carnivorous plants get their energy from converting sunlight to sugars in their leaves, just like any plants, by the process called photosynthesis. But they get some or most of their nutrients from the insects and small animals that that they trap. Most carnivorous plants live in nutrient-poor ground, like acidy bogs or rocky areas. Where plants in richer soil get nutrients through their roots, the plants in poor soil have to use other methods.

Nepenthes x pyriformis

Plants that eat animals and insects aren't all related. The ability to feed on living (or recently-living) creatures has evolved at least nine times in the plant world. Now there are over 580 species that scientists classify as carnivorous (meat-eating), and over 300 more that do some of the things true carnivorous plants do.

# WHERE THE PLANTS ARE

Most carnivorous plants live in areas with lots of sunlight. This allows some plants to have fewer leaves that use photosynthesis to convert sunlight into energy, and more leaves that help to trap animals and insects.

*Nepenthes rajah*

The plants tend to live in areas where the soil is water-logged, nutrient-poor, and very low on nitrogen and phosphorous. This cuts down on the number of competitor plant species that can survive in that area, but also means that the plants, that need nitrogen and phosphorous, have had to develop ways to get it.

Few plants evolve so they can eat meat. It is easier to get nutrients from the ground, through the roots. But plants that live in nutrient-poor soil need to find ways to get what the soil can't give them. They evolve so they can catch insects or even small birds, and they evolve ways to digest what they catch.

# CARNIVOROUS PLANT TYPES

Although carnivorous plants evolved in many different areas, plants around the world came up with similar methods and systems. Let's look at the various types:

**Drosera intermedia**

Pitfall Traps or Pitcher Plant

# PITFALL TRAPS

Pitfall traps are like little pitchers, brightly colored on the inside to look like flowers where an insect might harvest pollen. The plant may give off a scent like pollen. When an insect steps into the pitcher it finds, usually too late, that the pitcher walls are very slippery. The insect slides down into the sticky liquid at the bottom of the pitcher, and the chemicals there break the insect down so the plant can use its nutrients.

Plants of this sort often live in high-rainfall areas, and they usually develop a little drain or escape opening near the top of the pitcher so the plant does not fill so far up with rain water that the bugs that fall into it can float to safety.

Nepentheses mirabilis

# Butterworts Pinguicula

# FLYPAPER TRAPS

The trapping leaves of flypaper traps have many little glands that produce a gluey substance to catch an insect that lands there. On many of these plants, the leaves can roll up quite quickly to further capture the insect. Other chemicals in the leaf then slowly break down the insect so the plant can absorb its nutrients.

# SNAP TRAPS

The two main snap traps are the Venus flytrap and the waterwheel plant. They basically have a trapping area in two halves, as if you held your two hands side by side, with the palms up and your little fingers touching.

Waterwheel Plant

Venus fly trap showing trigger hairs

The inner surfaces of the trap have little sensory hairs, and those hairs have a simple memory. If something touches one of those hairs just once—nothing happens. But if there are two touches within a short period, the the trap slams shut on whatever has been walking around on it. The action is quite fast, taking about half a second. Then the plant can take all the time it wants to digest the insect.

## BLADDER TRAPS

**B**ladderworts use these traps on very small insects. These water plants have a process that pumps water out of their bladders, leaving an area of lower pressure that is sealed by a sort of trap door. There are some guard hairs to sense when an insect is near to the door.

Bladderwort

When the moment is right or the insect actually steps on the door, the trap door opens. The relative vacuum inside the bladder sucks in water from outside, and the insect along with it, and then the trap door shuts again. Then the bladderwort can digest what it has caught.

# LOBSTER-POT TRAPS

Lobster-pot traps have an opening that is easy to get into, but hard to get back out of. Many of these plants have inward-pointing hairs that force an insect that has started into the trap to keep on going forward. Eventually it reaches the bottom of the trap, where the digestive fluids wait.

**Nepenthes Northiana**

# COMBINATION PLANTS

Some carnivorous plants have multiple features. The sundew combines flypaper stickiness and snap-trap speed.

Sundew catching insect

Sundew – Drosera Capensis

# ALMOST-CARNIVOROUS PLANTS

There are some plants that trap and benefit from insects, without actually having a direct way to dissolve and digest them. There is a species of sundew with sticky leaves that attracts and catches insects.

The benefit to the plant is when another insect, the assassin bug, comes along and eats the insects the plant has trapped, like taking treats off a plate. Then the assassin bug excretes while it is on or near the plant, the excreted material makes the soil richer, and the plant benefits from the added nutrients in the soil. This seems like a way of getting food that would require you to be very, very patient, and not mind having bugs stuck all over you!

# A CARNIVOROUS PLANT IN THE HOUSE?

Could you grow a carnivorous plant in your house or garden? You can, but it takes special conditions, and some carnivorous plants live with humans better than others. Venus flytraps are guests in more than a few houses because of their interesting color and shape, and the fascinating way they deal with flies.

In general, for no matter what species of carnivorous plant, you have to take these factors into account:

**WATER:** you can't use tap water on a carnivorous plant, because the water is too rich in nutrients. You have to used distilled water or rain water, or you will basically overfeed the plant in a way it cannot tolerate.

**SOIL:** In general, these plants like nutrient-poor soil. You can't just stick them in the same soil mixture that you would use for a traditional house plant. A 3:1 mixture of peat moss and sharp horticultural sand is probably what most of these plants will appreciate.

Peat moss

**HUMIDITY:** Lots of these plants live in humid areas, so they don't do well in a dry house. If you have the plant in a pot, and the pot sitting in a shallow bowl of small stones, and you keep the small stones covered with water (and this can be tap water), that arrangement should provide enough humidity to please the plant.

**DIET:** Carnivorous plants outdoors will generally find and attract enough insects to keep themselves happy. A plant that catches no insects for a long while will probably not die, although it may not grow much or look very healthy.

If you don't have much fly activity in your house, and you have an indoors carnivorous plant, you may need to catch some bugs outdoors and feed them to the plant by hand (or with tweezers). But don't give the plant hamburger or pepperoni from your pizza! The plant won't know what to do with it, and the meat will just sit there until it rots, or may actually damage the plant.

**LIGHT:** Most carnivorous plants do best under bright sunlight, and this also helps strengthen their vivid, insect-attracting colors.

**TEMPERATURE:** Carnivorous plants grow in many climate zones, and some are pretty hardy. Some gardeners create a year-round bog garden for carnivorous plants and other bog species, even in areas where the temperature drops below zero in the winter.

**EXERCISE:** This is the last thing your plant needs! Don't tease the Venus flytrap to watch it snap shut, or poke at other varieties to see their leaves curl around the insect that isn't there. In general, keep in mind that plants, even carnivorous ones, are not designed to be as playful and fun as kittens. While a kitten may enjoy being stimulated over and over, your Venus flytrap may respond by dying.

# A WORLD OF SURPRISES

Nature is full of inventions and surprises. Read on in other Baby Professor books, like Who Lives in the Barren Desert?, to learn more about the plants and animals that share our Earth with us.

Made in the USA
San Bernardino, CA
24 June 2020